Tickle Day

Poems from Father Goose

by
Charles Ghigna

Illustrations by
Cyd Moore

Hyperion Books for Children
New York

ACKNOWLEDGMENTS

Some of the poems in *Tickle Day* first appeared in the magazines listed below. The author wishes to thank the publishers and editors of those publications for their permission to include the poems in this anthology. A few of the poems have been retitled and revised since their first publication. All of the poems in *Tickle Day* are copyright Charles Ghigna.

"A Rainy Day Sunrise," *Jack and Jill*, Apr. 1988.

"Clouds," *Children's Digest*, Feb. 1988.

"Tickle Day," *Humpty Dumpty*, Jan. 1991.

"If You Were," *Spark!*, Feb. 1994.

"One Thing That I Wonder," *Lollipops*, Mar. 1989.

"Happy Birthday, May!" *Humpty Dumpty*, Apr. 1985 and May 1990.

"Little Daddy Longlegs," *Turtle*, Mar. 1992.

"Looking at Fireflies," *Children's Playmate*, June 1984.

"The Bee Poem," *Jack and Jill*, Mar. 1990.

"Autumn," *Lollipops*, Nov. 1989.

"Family Tree," *Children's Digest*, Feb. 1987.

"Mother of the Night," *Humpty Dumpty*, Apr. 1984.

"The Peeker of the House," *Turtle*, Dec. 1988.

"The Silent Snow," *Children's Playmate*, Dec. 1988.

"Tomorrow's My Birthday," *Turtle*, Mar. 1992.

"Making Faces," *Lollipops*, Nov. 1991.

"Nature's Shows," *Jack and Jill*, Feb. 1987.

"A Poem Is a Little Path," *Jack and Jill*, Mar. 1992.

A special thanks to Howard Reeves, Andrea Cascardi, Liz Gordon, Jeanne McDermott, Lauren Wohl, Ellen Friedman, Joann Lovinski, Cecile Goyette, Lekha Menon, and all our friends at Hyperion Books for Children for their good faith in *Tickle Day*; to my beloved wife and best friend, Debra; to my precious treasures of love and inspiration, my children, Chip and Julie; and to the most creative kid in the whole world, my mother, Patricia Ghigna. —C.G.

FIRST EDITION

1 3 5 7 9 10 8 6 4 2

Library of Congress Cataloging-in-Publication Data

Ghigna, Charles. Tickle Day: poems from Father Goose / by Charles Ghigna; illustrated by Cyd Moore— 1st ed.   p.   cm.   Summary: Original poems and rhymes celebrating nature. ISBN 0-7868-0015-1 (trade)—ISBN 0-7868-2010-1 (lib. bdg.)   1. Nature—Juvenile poetry.   2. Children's poetry, American.   [1. Nature—Poetry. 2. American poetry.]   I. Moore, Cyd, ill.   II. Title. PS3557.H5F38   1994 811'.54—dc20   93-40847   CIP   AC

The artwork for each picture is prepared using watercolor and colored pencil.
This book is set in 16-point Della Robbia.
Book design by Joann Hill Lovinski.

For my son, Chip
—C.G.

For my son, Lindsay
—C.M.

The greatest poem ever known
Is one all poets have outgrown,
The poetry, innate, untold,
Of being only four years old.

—Christopher Morley

 Contents

A Rainy Day Sunrise

I wake up in the morning
But the sun is still asleep.
I see raindrops on my window
And gray clouds dark and deep.

I look inside my closet
Beneath my shoes and socks.
I find my brand-new drawing pad
Beside my crayon box.

I choose the color yellow.
I draw a shining sun.
I hang it in my window—
My day has now begun.

Each Shadow Has Its Sunshine

Each shadow has its sunshine.
Each rainbow has its rain.
Each sunrise has its sunset
So it can come again.

Each songbird has its silence.
Each nighttime has its day.
Each thornbush has its rosebud.
Each December has its May.

Each beginning has its ending.
Each ending has its start.
Each comes and goes because it knows
Each has its counterpart.

Clouds

Clouds are fluffy, puffy things
That drift across the sky.
They fill our eyes with fairy tales
Whenever they pass by.

Some look like boats and sailing ships,
Sometimes a swan or queen.
The sky is full of fantasy,
It's nature's movie screen.

Come see the many magic scenes
In heaven's demonstration.
It only takes a glance on high—
And your imagination.

Gesundheit!

My kite got caught
Up in the trees—
It happened when
The breeze sneezed!

Daydreaming

Out in the woods
Behind my house
Where no one goes
(Except a mouse),

I've made myself
A hiding place
Where no one knows
My name or face.

That's where I go
Each day to dream
Out in the sun
Beside my stream.

I close my eyes
And let the breeze
Come carry me
Beyond the trees.

I dream about
The jets I'll fly
Beyond the clouds
Across the sky.

I dream about
My flying soon
Beyond the earth
Up to the moon.

I dream about
My trips to Mars
Beyond the glow
Of evening stars.

I dream about
A world of fun
Beyond the sight
Of earth and sun.

I dream each day,
And just like you
I'll dream until
My dreams come true.

Tickle Day

Listen to the little laugh
That wakes up in your eyes.
It's a giggle that has gotten loose
To say to you, "Surprise!"

It's a warm and cozy feeling
Trying to come through.
It's the tickle of the morning
Rising inside you.

Sunbrella

I have a new umbrella
Of gold and green and white,
But every time I go outside
The rain stays out of sight.

My mother says on sunny days
I still might find it fun
To open my umbrella
And keep away the sun.

And so I walk with shadows
Upon my smiling face
Because my new *sun*brella
Goes with me *every*place!

If You Were

If you were a shining star
And I were your midnight,
I'd let you shine above me,
You'd be my only light.

If you were a scoop of ice cream
And I were an ice-cream cone,
I'd put you on my shoulders
And hold you for my own.

If you were the hands of time
And I were a grandfather clock,
I'd let you spin around with me,
Together we'd ticktock.

If you were the pages of a book
And I were reading you,
I'd read as slow as I could go
So I never would get through.

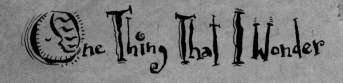

One Thing That I Wonder

One thing that I wonder
Is why the world is round
And why the trees grow toward the sky
Instead of underground.

One thing that I wonder
Is how it came to be
That elephants live on the ground
While birds live in a tree.

One thing that I wonder
Is why the sky is blue,
Why spiders all have eight legs
While we have only two.

One thing that I wonder
Is how it came to be
That cats are quick to sleep in laps
While whales sleep in the sea.

One thing that I wonder
Is why we wonder why
About the things that roam the earth
And fill the sea and sky.

Happy Birthday, May!

I opened the window
And in stepped May,
Bringing a party
For her birthday.

She brought roses
And tulips
And strawberry pie.

She brought robins
And chipmunks
And squirrels that fly.

She brought puppies
And rainbows
And kittens that mew.

She brought sunshine
And picnics
And pigeons that coo.

She brought crickets
And bluebirds
And beetles that sing.

She brought buttercup
Cakes
With creamy icing.

She brought all the things
A May day can bring.
She brought in herself—
She brought in Spring.

Little Daddy Longlegs

Little Daddy Longlegs played in the sun,
Climbing up the front steps just for fun.
One leg, two legs, three legs, four,
Eight legs later he was at my door.

He sat on the mat looking up at me,
Till I opened the door an inch or three.
I caught him in a jelly jar just for fun
And put him in the window in the morning sun.

But Little Daddy Longlegs curled up small,
Looking like he wasn't even there at all.
He just sat still looking up at me,
So I opened the jar and set him free.

Little Daddy Longlegs played in the sun,
Climbing down the front steps just for fun.
One leg, two legs, three legs, four,
Eight legs later he was there no more.

Looking at Fireflies

Like little flying flashlights,
The fireflies come out
To brighten up the nighttime
When summer comes about.

They light up every pine tree
Like a Christmas in July
And welcome all their night friends
To a dance beneath the sky.

They spin and dive and make a show.
They waltz across the lawn.
They wink and blink their little lights
Until their glow is gone.

So next time after dinner
When you're walking by the park,
Come watch the friendly fireflies—
They're dancing in the dark.

The Bee Poem

A poem is a busy bee
Buzzing in your head.
His hive is full of hidden thoughts
Waiting to be said.

His honey comes from your ideas
That he makes into rhyme.
He flies around just looking for
What goes on in your mind.

When it is time to let him out
To make some poetry,
He gathers up your deepest thoughts
And then he sets them free.

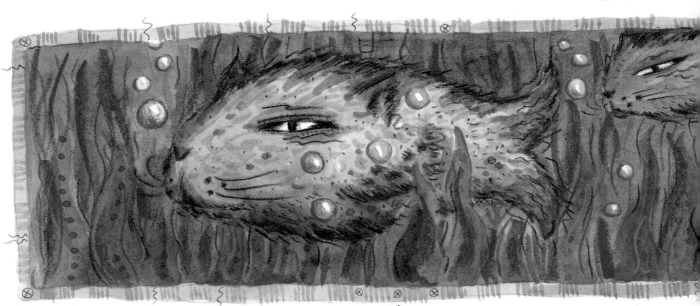

Catfish Aren't Furry

*Cat*fish aren't furry.
Bald eagles don't lose hair.
I've never heard a *buzzard* buzz
While flying through the air.

Fiddler crabs don't fiddle.
Sea *horses* have no feet.
Sea *cows* don't know how to moo
And *cheet*ahs never cheat.

*Bull*frogs have no set of horns.
Flying fish don't soar.
Dande*lions* aren't fierce,
That's why they never roar!

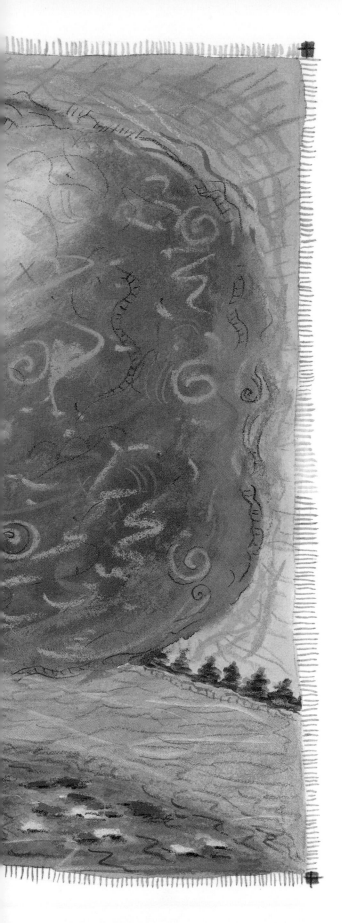

On The Way To School

I'll tell you why I'm tardy
And I hope my excuse will do.
I stopped to view upon a leaf
A spider and some dew.

She spun a web before my eyes
With a soft and silver hue,
And when she looked, I looked at her
And whispered, "Peekaboo!"

I think I may have startled her
And so I waved good-bye,
But when I turned around to go,
I met a butterfly!

I almost caught him in my hand
To bring to class for you,
But when I tried to peek inside,
Away my treasure flew.

And that is how I'm tardy,
But I had to tell you why.
It's all the fault of a spider's web
And a sneaky butterfly.

 Autumn

The time of year
That I like best
Is when the world
Is color-blessed,

When trees put on
Their brightest clothes
And chilly winds
Light up my nose,

When playful days
Are turned inside
And families feast
At fireside,

Before snowflakes
Begin to fall
And sleds and snowmen
Have a ball.

It's always fun
This time of year
When autumn comes
And winter's near.

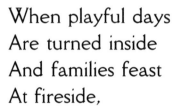

24

Family Tree

My roots are deep within you,
Growing as you grow.
My shade provides the shelter
For the new seeds that you sow.

No matter what the season
I stand here just the same.
Come winter, spring, or summer,
My branches bear your name.

Mother of the Night

The moon watches over us
Like a Mother of the Night.
She sees through the darkness
With her soft and silvery light.

She peeks in on each one of us
And watches as we dream,
Gently placing kisses
With every new moonbeam.

She covers us with shadows
As she tiptoes 'cross the sky.
She checks on all her children
As she slowly passes by.

26

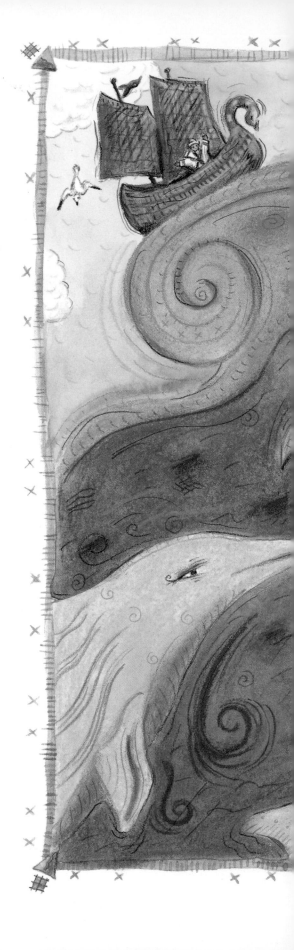

The Sneeze Cruise

Mother says it's nap time,
But I pretend it's not.
I climb into my bed and I
Pretend that it's a yacht.

I sail away to where I want,
To islands in the sun,
To emerald seas out in the breeze
Where daydreams like to run.

I ride the waves all up and down
With dolphins at my side,
And sea gulls flying overhead
Serving as my guide.

And when it's time to leave behind
Imaginary skies,
I simply set my sights for home—
And open up my eyes!

The Peeker of the House

Who gets to go to the window first?
Who gets to see the snow?
Who gets to go to the window first
And hear the cold wind blow?

Who gets to go to the window first
And see first signs of spring?
Who gets to go to the window first
And hear the robin sing?

Who gets to go to the window first
And see the summer moon?
Who gets to go to the window first
And hear the crickets' tune?

Who gets to go to the window first
And watch the falling leaves?
Who gets to go to the window first
And hear the autumn breeze?

Who gets to go to the window first
And tell us what's to see?
Who gets to go to the window first—
Look out world—it's me!

Bubbles

A bubble is a magic ball,
A globe of light both big and small,
A soapy sphere of bathtub fun,
A foamy wave out in the sun.

A bubble is a world of joy,
A free and fragile little toy,
A tiny shining clear balloon
Floating by just like the moon.

Bubbles, bubbles everywhere,
Balls of magic in the air,
Drifting bright beneath the sun,
Bubbles fill the world with fun.

The Silent Snow

While we're sleeping
Snowflakes fall
From the heavens
To us all.

Trees and fields
Fill up with snow
Till everything
Is all aglow.

When we wake up
All is white—
A gift sent from
The silent night.

Turtle Trouble

Tell me if you think you know
How to make a turtle go.
I've pushed, I've tapped,
I've really tried—
But mine, I think,
Is stuck inside!

Would You Like to Meet a Ewe?

Would you like to meet an aye-aye?
Would you like to meet a gnu?
Would you like to meet a Brahma bull,
A kinkajou or two?

Would you like to meet a marten?
Would you like to meet a lynx?
Would you like to meet a bunch of skunks
Minus all their stinks?

Would you like to meet a kiwi?
Would you like to meet a ewe?
Would you like to meet these furry friends?
Then let's go to the zoo!

Tomorrow's My Birthday

Tomorrow's my birthday
And I'll be four,
And I won't have
To stay home anymore.

I'll take down my bank
Right off my shelf
And I will go out
And about by myself.

I'll buy me a ticket
And I'll take a train
And I'll go to Texas
To ride on the range.

I'll buy me some boots
And a hat, but no toys,
'Cause I'll be as big
As all the cowboys.

I'll rope and I'll ride
And I'll be the best
Of all the cowboys
In the world and the West.

And when it gets dark
On the cattle drive—
Well, maybe I'll wait
Until I am five.

Making Faces

Draw a big circle,
Put a nose in place,
Add two ears
To your funny face.

Long hair, short hair
On its head?
Black hair, blond hair,
Brown or red?

Blue eyes, brown eyes,
Glasses or not,
Give it a smile
And what have you got?

A lady? A man?
A boy or a girl?
A bald-headed daddy?
A baby with a curl?

Look at the face
That you drew.
Now look in the mirror—
Is it you?

Nature's Shows

Nature puts on little shows
Every time it rains or snows.

Drumrolls of a thunderstorm
Marching spring in to perform,

Tap dances of summer rain
Playing on the windowpane,

Somersaulting autumn leaves
Spinning through the silent breeze:

Nature's shows are quite a sight.
Her final curtain, snowy white.

It's Snow Wonder!

It's snow wonder that we cheer
Snowflakes when they fall each year.

It's snow wonder snowmen grow
From our garden made of snow.

It's snow wonder that we skate
Across the lake a figure eight.

It's snow wonder that we slide
Sleds across the countryside.

It's snow wonder that we play
Winter games each snowy day.

It's snow wonder that we sleep
Snuggled warm in blankets deep.

Mother Nature

I walk among the daffodils.
I talk among the trees.
I sing among the mockingbirds.
I ride upon the breeze.

I float among the flakes of snow.
I swim in every stream.
The earth and sky are where I roam,
And all that's in between.

Winter, spring, summer, fall,
I journey day and night.
I cover every countryside
With green and gold and white.

A Poem Is a Little Path

A poem is a little path
That leads you through the trees.
It takes you to the cliffs and shores,
To anywhere you please.

Follow it and trust your way
With mind and heart as one,
And when the journey's over,
You'll find you've just begun.